A Handy Guide to Su

your NEW LIFE

DR ELEWECHI NGOZI OKIKE

Copyright © 2016 Elewechi Ngozi Okike

British Library Cataloguing in Publication Data

All rights reserved. No part of this work may be reproduced or stored in an information retrieval system (other than for purposes of review) without the express permission of the publisher in writing.

A catalogue record for this book is available from the British Library.

ISBN 978-0-955 9361-5-9

Published by Assurance Publications Ltd,
P.O. Box 112, Washington, NE37 1YB
United Kingdom

Tel/Fax: 0845 299 1127; 07799653641

Email: info@assurancepublications.com
http://www.assurancepublications.com

Produced for Assurance Publications by
Assurance Publishers
Cover and Content Design by
Kenteba Kreations
www.kentebakreations.com

FOREWORD

In Matthew 28:18-20, Jesus told His disciples, "All authority has been given to Me in heaven and on earth. Go therefore and make disciples of all the nations, baptizing them in the name of the Father and of the Son and of the Holy Spirit, teaching them to observe all things that I have commanded you; and lo, I am with you always, even to the end of the age." (NKJV)

These were the last words of Jesus to his disciples before His ascension. He was giving to His disciples final instructions in relation to how to build people spiritually in the church.

On the subject of church life there are countless books that have been published, many seminars to attend and church conferences arranged. The 'Body of Christ' is not devoid of teaching in relation to what the church needs and much of it is excellent revelation and we need to thank God that we live in a day when such teaching is readily available. Having acknowledged that we must never forget the words Jesus said to his disciples in those final moments. Make disciples and teach them to obey my commands'. This suggests that people are not born disciples but that they need to enter a process by which they will become disciples. Jesus knew the importance and impact of a life touching another life. Therefore it is vital that we who have already submitted our own will and are true disciples give ourselves to the process of building people, so that they in turn will do the same to others. We were not told to gather a crowd and use the techniques of the day to accomplish that aim; this is not about how many people we can gather on a Sunday but how effective we are in making people true followers of Jesus Christ.

Ngozi Okike is a woman who all her life has understood these principles. Her desire is to see the 'Body of Christ' built up and a lifestyle to begin the moment a person surrenders his/her life to Christ, so that it will ultimately produce true discipleship in their lives. Because of her deep conviction and belief that a person should be taught to lean upon the Lord and know what He is commanding us to do she has given us (the church) this tool by which we can achieve this objective in people's lives.

I have known Ngozi Okike for many years and know that before she penned anything in this manual she has lived through it and tested it in her own life. You will find that this manual is very basic and written in plain easy to understand language so as not to alienate anyone from the truth. Ngozi herself is highly educated and has been involved in the higher education sector for over 33 years; yet she has been able to communicate life changing principles in a style that all will understand.

This manual is a vital tool for those who desire to fulfill the commission of Jesus Christ to 'Make disciples and teach them to obey My commands'. It is also a handy guide for new believers who desire to live a successful Christian life.

Pastor Ken Gott
Bethshan Church
Tyne & Wear, United Kingdom

PREFACE

It is often said that the journey of a thousand miles begins with the first step. Sometimes people who set out on a journey fail to get to their destinations, either because of an accident or other unforeseen circumstances. Just as it is in the physical realm, so also it is in the spiritual. Inviting Jesus into their lives is the first step in the Christian journey for new believers. The purpose of this book is to ensure that they arrive at their 'destination' safely.

This book, which has been inspired by the Holy Spirit, has been written out of a strong desire to see new believers established in God. Imagine a person who has spent years in prison, who on his or her release opens the prison doors and looks out into the world of the unknown. The sun is shining brightly, but he or she does not know which way to turn. Like a person providing a sense of direction and guidance to such a prisoner, so also is this book designed to provide direction and guidance for new believers.

Jesus prayed that we should bear fruits and that our fruits should remain. It is my prayer that any new believer who gets hold of this book will not be in any doubt as to what the Christian life entails. Every church, Christian group or organization that is passionate about seeing souls saved and nurtured in the faith should find this book an invaluable tool.

I pray that the Lord will help every believer who reads this book to go on to maturity and help others find Christ.

Ngozi Okike

DEDICATION

To the glory of God, this book is dedicated to all those souls who will confess with their mouths the Lord Jesus, believe in their hearts that God raised Him from the dead, and receive Him into their lives, as their personal Lord and Saviour.

It is also dedicated to all those who faithfully heed the command of the Lord to 'go... and make disciples of all nations ... teaching them to observe all things' that the Lord has commanded.

ACKNOWLEDGEMENTS

This book would not have been possible without the support and encouragement of the many vessels that God used to make it happen.

Firstly, I want to thank the Lord Jesus for all that He means to me, and for all that He has accomplished, is accomplishing and will yet accomplish in my life. It is His inspiration and my deep love for Him that led to the writing of this book.

Also, I'd like to thank my pastors, Ken and Lois Gott, for their passion to see souls saved and effectively discipled. This desire led to the decision to provide a tool for the church to use to make effective discipleship a reality.

Our daughter, Adaeze, did most of the typing of the manuscript, including providing useful insights and helpful suggestions. She's such a treasure. Thanks also to Mabel Kazimanyi for her help with some typing. I would like to thank our son, Helmut, for his suggestions which helped shape the new design for the 2nd edition of this book.

Special thanks too, to Joojo Kyei-Sarpong (Kenteba Kreations) for the graphic designs, and every thing he did to get this 2nd edition ready for publication.

I am extremely grateful to him. Last, but not the least, I would like to thank my husband, Chikezie Okike, for his support and encouragement over the years, and for allowing me to be who God created me to be. I shall always remain grateful to him for his love and support.

CONTENTS

Foreword .... *iv*

Preface .... *vi*

Dedication .... *vii*

Acknowledgements .... *viii*

1.	A New Beginning	11
2.	Growing in Grace	23
3.	Part of a Family	34
4.	Relationships	38
5.	Share your Faith	42
6.	One with Christ	44
7.	You shall receive Power	50
8.	Run, Fight ... to Win	53
9.	Extend the Kingdom through Giving	61
10.	The Old and the New Life	64
11.	How to Deal with Temptation	72
12.	Getting Back Your Fight	82
13.	Prayer and Fasting	86
14.	Keys for Successful Christian Living	90
15.	Where to find Help	93

x

1
A NEW BEGINNING

Congratulations!
You have taken that great step of inviting Jesus into your life as your personal Lord and Saviour. I want you to know that by taking that step, you have made the best and the most important decision in your life, and I would like to welcome you into the family of God. You have now become a member of the Body of Christ, the Royal Family of God. You are now a citizen of God's Kingdom. You no longer belong to the Kingdom of darkness, but have now been translated into God's Kingdom of light.

Now that you are saved, you are a Child of God with certain rights and privileges, which you need to be aware of. More importantly, your Father God wants you to enjoy your life everyday – to the full. This is why Jesus said in John 10:10 "...I came that they may have and enjoy life, and have it in abundance (to the full, until it overflows)" (Amplified Bible).

A NEW BEGINNING

This book has been written to help you live your new life to the full as a member of God's holy family.

> *But as many as received Him, to them He gave the right to become children of God, to those who believe in His name.*
> **John 1: 12**

What Happened to You?

Perhaps you might still be confused about the steps you have just taken, or that you took recently. The point is this; you were a sinner, condemned to die, and on your way to hell.

For in Romans 3:23, the Bible declares that *"ALL have sinned and fall short of the glory of God"*. And in Romans 6: 23, it says, *"the wages (price) of sin is death"*. Also, 1 John1: 8-9 says "if we say we have no sin, we deceive ourselves, and the truth is not in us. If we confess our sins, he is faithful and just to forgive us our sins, and to cleanse us from all unrighteousness". This is why, before you received Jesus into your life as your personal Lord and Saviour, you had to first **ADMIT** you were a sinner; you **BELIEVED** that Jesus paid the price for your sins, and you **CONFESSED** your sins. Lastly, you **DECIDED** to make Him Lord (put Him in charge) of your life. This is the A, B, C, D of Salvation.

A NEW BEGINNING   14

Happy Birthday!

Having said the prayer of confession and invited Jesus into your life, you have become 'born again'. For in John 3:3 Jesus says *"...unless a person is born again (anew, from above), he cannot ever see (know, be acquainted with, and experience) the kingdom of God"*. (Amplified Bible).

The day or moment you made that decision is very special. You should note the date in your diary, and always remember it as your 'birthday'; the day you were born into the family of God. Many Christians do celebrate that day. And, just as there is rejoicing and celebration when a child is born into the world, there is also celebration when a person gets saved, i.e. gets born again (Luke 15:7).

So, there was a celebration in heaven when you confessed your sins and invited Jesus into your heart.

"... there is joy in the presence of the angels of God over one sinner who repents"
Luke 15:10

YOUR NEW LIFE   15

Brand New Person

Now that you have been born again, you have been saved from God's wrath and judgement that will be the portion of those who reject Christ. You are now a member of a different family. Once you belonged to the kingdom of darkness, but now you belong to the Kingdom of Light. You cannot live your life as you used to. For the Bible says in 2Corinthians 5: 17 *"when someone becomes a Christian s(he) becomes a BRAND NEW PERSON inside. S(h)e is not the same any more. A NEW LIFE HAS BEGUN!"* (Living Bible).

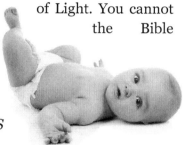

You are now a new person in Christ. And as a new child born into the world has to be fed and looked after to grow into a normal healthy child, so also you must be fed and nurtured so that you can become a healthy and vibrant Christian. The spiritual food of the Christian is the Word of God, the Bible. You must read it everyday to grow. 1Peter 2: 2-3 says *"as new born babes, desire the sincere milk of the Word, that you may grow thereby: if indeed you have tasted that the Lord is gracious"* (NKJB).

You cannot survive in your new life if you do not feed (i.e. read, meditate, reflect) on, the Word of God. By doing so you will be able to resist all the devil will throw at you. If you do not have a Bible, you need to get one. It would be one of the best presents you have ever bought for yourself.

Watch Out!

Whilst it is true that by inviting Jesus into your life you made the best decision in life, you must also realise that you have also made someone, the devil, angry. When you derailed from the kingdom of darkness into God's kingdom, you reduced the number of people going to hell, and the devil will do everything within his power to get you back. Just as no mother would sit back and watch a stranger snatch her precious child from her hands, so also, the devil will not sit back and let you go easily. He is going to put up a fight to get you back. Because he is so evil, he does not want any one saved from hell, or from God's wrath. He wants as many people as possible in hell with him. So, you have to do all you can to resist ALL his attempts to get you back into his fold.

"Be sober, be vigilant; because your adversary the devil, as a roaring lion, walks about, seeking whom he may devour"
1Peter 5: 8

No Condemnation

One of the most familiar ways the devil will attack you is through your thoughts.

He would want to confuse you, to accuse you, and to remind you of all your past sins. He would bring guilt feelings on you again and again. Therefore, you need to arm yourself with the Word of God. Romans 8:1 says, "there is therefore now no condemnation for those who are in Christ Jesus". And in Isaiah 44:22, God declares to you, "I have caused your transgressions to vanish like a cloud and your sins as a fog ..." The blood of Jesus has washed away your past sins. Also, in Isaiah 43:25, God says, "I, yes, I alone am he who blots away your sins for my own sake and will never think of them again (Living Bible). Therefore, do not allow the devil to taunt you with your past. Again, in Phil.3: 13-14, we are admonished to forget the things, which are behind, and to reach out for those things which lie ahead. We are to press toward the mark for the prize of the high calling of God in Christ Jesus. There is nothing you can do about what has happened in the past. God has taken care of all your past mistakes, failures, hurts, disappointments and so on. You can press forward and embrace this new life in God.

Tell Someone

One of the best things you can do for yourself is to tell someone what has happened to you. Begin with your immediate family and friends. Tell them that you are now born again and a member of God's holy family. 1Peter 2: 9-10 says, "But you are a chosen generation, a royal priesthood, a holy nation, His own special people, that you may proclaim the praises of Him who called you out of darkness into His marvelous light; who once were not a people but are now the people of God, who had not obtained mercy but now have obtained mercy" (New King James Bible). It is no small thing to belong to God's family; it is no small thing to be saved from hell, from God's eternal judgement. If you escaped an accident, you would not keep it to yourself, would you? If you won the lottery, would you not throw a Champagne party? Well, being saved, born again, is much more than winning the lottery. For, no matter how much you win in the lottery, if you should die suddenly, you would not carry any of it (or indeed any other possession) with you. But being saved means escaping eternal judgement; as Hebrews 9:27 says, "And just as it is destined that men die once, and after that comes judgement". There is a very interesting story in John 4 about a woman of Samaria who met Jesus at the Well, and from that single encounter, she got her whole village saved. You may not get a whole village saved in one go, like she did, but you can start somewhere by simply sharing how your life has been radically changed.

"One of the two who heard John speak, and followed Him, was Andrew, Simon Peter's brother. He first found his own brother Simon, and said to him, 'We have found the Messiah ...' And he brought him to Jesus"

John 1: 40-42

Remember, it is as simple as A, B, C, D:

A – <u>Admit</u> you are a sinner; for the Bible says *'ALL have sinned and come short of the glory of God' and that the wages of sin is DEATH' (Romans 3:10, 23; 6:23)*. So, whether any one believes it or not, the Bible says all men are sinners.

B – <u>Believe</u> *that Jesus paid the price for your sins. God made a Way for the salvation of everyman through the death of Christ on the Cross; and there is no other way (John 3:16; John 14:6; Acts 4:12; Romans 5:1-12)*

C – <u>Confess</u> *your sins to God and ask Him to forgive you. The Bible says, 'if we say we have no sin, we deceive ourselves ...' but if we confess our sins, He is faithful and just to forgive us our sins and to cleanse us from all unrighteousness' (1 John 1: 8-9; Isaiah 43:25)*

D – <u>Decide</u> to make Him Lord (put Him in charge) of your life. Give up your evil ways and accept the new life that He gives. The Bible says *"if anyone is in Christ, s(he) is a new creation; old things have passed away; behold, all things have become new" (2 Corinthians 5:14-17)*.

Use the following pages to help you make some notes that you may find helpful.

A NEW BEGINNING

Notes

1. Write the following:

   (i) The day you got saved

   _____

   _____

   (ii) Where you got saved

   _____

   (iii) The name and contact details of the person who helped you to get saved (if known)

   _____

   _____

   _____

   _____

   _____

2. Write down the names of a few people you may want to tell about your salvation:

   _____

   _____

YOUR NEW LIFE

3. Make a note of some of the important things in this chapter that you want to reflect on:

_____

_____

_____

_____

_____

_____

_____

_____

_____

_____

4. Do you have a Bible? If you do not have one, make a note of when you would get one and where you would get it from:

_____

_____

_____

_____

_____

A NEW BEGINNING

5. What does the Bible say in 2 Corinthians 5: 17? What does this mean to you as a new believer?

6. You might find this declaration helpful.

DECLARATION

I am a child of God. The devil has no power over me, no unsettled claims against me. Everything has been settled through the death of Jesus, the Son of God, on the Cross. I am now a new person in Christ. I am no longer the person I used to be. I will no longer live in the condemnation of my past. Praise God all my sins have been washed away, and my name has been written in the Book of Life.

2
GROWING IN GRACE

Imagine a baby born and not fed, would he or she grow? Probably not! Earlier, I did mention that the spiritual food of a Christian is the Bible, the Word of God.

If you do not read your Bible every day, you will be starving your spirit man, and it may die! It is like putting a seed on fresh soil and not watering it, or giving it necessary nourishment. It would whither and die. Therefore, if you are very sincere about the decision you made to invite Jesus into your life, you must feed (i.e. read, meditate and act) on the Word of God. Its importance cannot be over-emphasised.

Developing Intimacy

One of the things I enjoy to watch is a mother playing with, and talking to her little baby. Isn't it amazing that although little babies literally cannot speak, their mothers always speak to them, and understand "their language" even if that language is only "noise" to the ears?

Now, imagine a child born, fed, and just left in the cot or pram on his or her own. The child has no other contact or show of affection from the mother. This child would suffer from emotional imbalance.

Research carried out by some psychologists on babies and young children demonstrate that children who are shown love and affection, and feel this sense of touch, grow healthier than those who had no form of touch or contact from anyone. Therefore, as it is in the natural, so it is in the spiritual. GOD IS NOW YOUR HEAVENLY FATHER. He loves you so much that He wants to spend time with you – ALONE! He needs that time to develop intimacy with you. This is why you find that mothers of young babies cannot go back to work immediately. They know their new babies need lots of time and attention to develop and grow into healthy children. So it is with you, in your new relationship with YOUR HEAVENLY FATHER, spend quality time with Him!

YOUR NEW LIFE

God Has Time For You!

The interesting thing is that GOD HAS ALL THE TIME IN THE WORLD FOR YOU. He is never too busy or tired like some mothers, who at the end of the day just want to put the child to sleep and get on with other things. God waits on you, and is willing to give you as much time as you are prepared to spend with Him.

"Study to show yourself approved unto God, as a workman who does not need to be ashamed, rightly dividing the word of truth"
2Timothy 2: 15

GROWING IN GRACE

Someone has said that "God is a Gentleman"; He never forces Himself on anyone and that is why He never created us like robots. Instead, He has given us a will – to choose. So, as a newborn babe in Christ, YOU MUST MAKE OUT TIME TO TALK TO YOUR HEAVENLY FATHER. This is known as PRAYING! It is also known as having fellowship with God. The more you talk to God, the more He talks to you, and the more you get to know and understand Him. Isn't it amazing how little babies recognise their mothers' voices, touch and so on? It is because of the intimate relationship that has being built between mother and child.

You must work hard on building your relationship with God. When you wake up every morning, remember to spend a few minutes with God to say "Thank you Father that I am alive and well to witness another day". Declare joyfully "this is the day that the Lord has made, I will rejoice and be glad in it". Personally, I like to have a worship song on when I am praying or spending time with God. Remember Jim Reeves' old classic – "We Thank Thee"? Once you put the music on, you hear him sing "we thank thee, each morning for a new born day..."

It is wonderful to have a thankful heart and to appreciate God's goodness in our lives.

Always start your day with God. Ask Him to guide and direct all you have to do each day. Never rush out of the presence of God!

YOUR NEW LIFE

God has all the time for you. You can talk to Him anytime, anywhere – in your car as you drive to work; on the bus, train, coach, airplane, whilst doing the dishes, jogging, in the bathroom – anywhere. Praying is an internal communication. Similarly, you can read your Bible anytime, including during your lunch break, as you take your sandwich!

It is often said that "a prayerless Christian, is a powerless Christian". If you want to know how to fight the devil, then you must be a prayerful Christian. If you know how to talk to your friends, then you can talk to God. He's not only your father, He wants to be your friend too – an intimate one for that matter.

Why Study the Word?

Earlier I mentioned the importance of reading the Bible in order to grow. Through the Bible, God speaks to you, and when you pray, you talk to God. How would you like to speak to someone who never responds to you?

When you read, study and meditate on the Word of God, the Bible, you discover the secrets of how to live a successful Christian life. It is through reading the Bible that we get to know God more intimately.

Here are just a few of the things that the Bible can mean to you:

1. Food for the Soul

Just as you need food to stay healthy and strong, so also do you as a believer need the word of God as food for your soul. It feeds your spirit-man. Here are what some Patriarchs of the Bible said about the Word of God. "I have treasured the words of His mouth more than my necessary food" (Job 23:12)

"How sweet are Your words to my taste, sweeter than honey to my mouth!" (David, in Psalm 119:103)

2. Give Guidance and Understanding

If you were traveling to a place that you have never been before, you would take a map with you, a satellite navigation system, or ask for direction from someone who knows the way. This is what the Bible will do for you as a new believer in Christ. You have started a journey with God, and you need guidance and direction. Also as you meditate on the word of God, you will find out how not to walk in disobedience or sin against God by doing the wrong things. The word of God will teach you what you need to know as a Child of God. Look at what these verses of the Bible have to say about this:

- *Your word is a lamp to my feet and a light to my path* (Psalm 119:105)

- *How can a young man cleanse his way? By taking heed according to Your word.* (Psalm 119:9)

- *Your word I have hidden in my heart that I might not sin against You.* (Psalm 119:11)

YOUR NEW LIFE

- *I have restrained my feet from every evil way, that I may keep Your word.* (Psalm 119:101)

- *Through Your precepts I get understanding; therefore I hate every false way.* (Psalm 119:104)

3. To Overcome Temptation

Remember I mentioned earlier that because you have decamped from the devil's camp, he is not going to make things easy. He will try to attack you in so many ways and tempt you with so many things, not only to discourage you, but to try to take you back into His camp. This is another reason why you need to study the Word of God. Did you know that even Jesus was tempted by the devil? If Our Lord was so tempted, you can be sure you will be tempted too. How did Jesus overcome temptation? See Matthew 4:1-11. He used the Word, saying each time to the devil, "it is written...". You also need to know the Word for yourself, so that when the devil comes to tempt you, you too can say "it is written...". If you do not know what the Word says about a particular temptation you are facing, you would not know what to say.

4. Comfort in Affliction

Besides the temptations of the enemy, you may face difficult and challenging times and you need to know that there is comfort in the Word. Here are a few scriptures about this:

- *"This is my comfort in my affliction for Your word has given me life"* (Psalm 119:50)

- *"I remembered Your judgments of old, O Lord and have comforted myself.* (Psalm 119:52)

5. More Precious than Silver and Gold

The Word of God is more precious than silver or gold, or any other treasures in this world. Even God says in His Word "heaven and earth will pass away, but my words will by no means pass away" (Matthew 24:35). Here are a few scriptures that confirm this:

- *"The law of your mouth is better to me than thousands of coins of gold and silver".* (Psalm 119:72)

- *"Therefore I love your commandments more than gold, yes than fine gold!"* (Psalm 119:127)

- *"I rejoice at your Word as one who finds great treasure"* (Psalm 119:162).

Besides, there are many promises that God your Father has made to you as His child and you will never discover them unless you read His word. Imagine a wealthy man who dies and leaves all his wealth and possessions in his Will for his children. They will never find out about their inheritance until they open their father's Will. So also it is with you; God has made so much provision for you in His word, the Bible. The only way you can find out what you are entitled to is by reading the word.

Be Doers of the Word

It is not enough for you to read and study the word. The Bible says you are to be a doer of the Word. The word will not benefit you if you do not apply it to your life. That is, your life needs

YOUR NEW LIFE

to be governed by the word of God. Hence James 1:22-25 says "but be doers of the word and not hearers only, deceiving yourselves. For if anyone is a hearer of the word and not a doer, he is like a man observing his natural face in a mirror; for he observes himself, goes away, and immediately forgets what kind of man he was. But he who looks into the perfect law of liberty and continues in it, and is not a forgetful hearer but a doer of the work, this one will be blessed in what he does (New King James Bible)."

Ask for God's Help

Sometimes you may not understand everything you read in the Bible. This is why it is helpful to pray and ask God to open your spiritual eyes so that the Holy Spirit will give you understanding of what you read and the grace to act on it. That is, to do what it says.

Notes

1. Make a note here of any new things you have learnt recently in your new faith and any questions you may wish to ask the person who led you to the Lord.

_____

_____

_____

GROWING IN GRACE

2. How will you organize your life to make sure you have time to pray and to study the word of God?

YOUR NEW LIFE **33**

3. Make a note of bible passages to memorize to help you each day of the week.

3
PART OF A FAMILY

When a child is born, s(he) is born into a family. I'm sure you know how horrible we all feel when we hear that a child has been abandoned somewhere by the mother. So also, when a person becomes born again, s(he) is part of one Big Family of believers. We talked a lot about this earlier.

Christian Fellowship

Just as no human being can survive alone, so also, no Christian can survive on his or her own. We are meant to support one another. Hence you need to be part of a "family". This means you should find a good Bible -believing church and join them in fellowship. How do I know which is a good church? Find out what Jesus said about this in Matthew 7:13-23. Ask the Lord to lead you to where He wants you to belong and He will. However, here are some things to look out for:

- Does the church believe that Jesus Christ is the Son of the Living God, the way, the Truth and the life?
- Does the church believe in the birth, death and resurrection of Christ?
- Does the church believe that the Bible is God's Holy Word?
- Does the church believe that Jesus is coming back again for His Bride, the Church?

One can go on and on about how to identify a good Bible-believing church. You would find that as you get to know God more intimately, He would reveal so much to you about Himself.

Also, when you join a church, do not be a Christian only on Sundays. In addition to the usual Sunday morning services, many churches have cell, home or in-house fellowship groups, weekly Bible study and prayer meetings. You should do your best to attend as many of these as possible to help you in your walk with God. Also, be an active member of your church and not just a spectator and allow God to use the gifts and talents He has deposited in you to bless others and to extend His Kingdom here on earth.

Joint Heir with Christ

As a believer, you are not just part of a family, but you are a child of God and a joint-heir with Christ. In John 1:12-13 the Bible declares that *"as many as received Him, to them He gave the right to become children of God, to those who believe in His name, who were born, not of blood, nor of the will of the flesh, nor of the will of man, but of God" (NKJV).*

This means you are entitled to all the rights and privileges of a child in God's kingdom (see Romans 8: 14-17). Do not be afraid to call God your Father, and to claim all that He has promised you in His word. Remember what we said about the word of God being His Will for you? As you study the Bible diligently, you will find out more about your inheritance.

Use these pages to write down some important notes about the church family to which you belong.

Notes

1. Have you found a good church yet? If you have, what are the name and the contact details of your church? Also write here the names of your pastors:

_____

_____

_____

_____

_____

2. Write here the time the church meets on Sunday mornings:

_____

_____

_____

_____

3. Write down the other days of the week that the church meets and the times, including the venue, if different from the venue for the Sunday morning services:

YOUR NEW LIFE

37

_____

_____

_____

_____

_____

_____

4. Write down the name of your cell or house group leader
   and the venue of your house fellowship or cell.

_____

_____

_____

_____

4
RELATIONSHIPS

One of the factors that will determine your success as a new believer is the type of relationships you keep from now on. You need to remember the following important principles:

- Every relationship has a spiritual dimension
- Some relationships are taking you closer to God or away from God
- Relationships are doors to your future.
- Your life is going at the pace of you closest relationships
- You can get to your destination in 10 seconds, 10 minutes, 10 hours, 10 days, 10 month or 10 years .... Which do you prefer?
- The type of people you hang around with will determine how soon you will get to your destination.

As a new Christian, you are not the same person you used to be. Therefore, if you were going out with people whose lives are contrary to the Word of God, then you need to take precaution. This is why the Bible says in 1 Corinthians 15: 33, 'do not be deceived and misled! Evil companionships (communion, associations) corrupt and deprave good manners and morals and character" (Amplified Bible).

Also 2 Corinthians 6: 14 – 7: 1 says

You are not the same as those who do not believe. So do not join yourselves to them. Good and bad do not belong together.

YOUR NEW LIFE 39

Light and darkness cannot share together. How can Christ and Belial, the devil have any agreement? What can a believer have together with a nonbeliever? The temple of God cannot have any agreement with idols, and we are the temple of the living God. As God said: "I will live with them and walk with them. And I will be their God and they will be my people". Leave those people, and be separate, says the Lord. Touch nothing that is unclean, and I will accept you." I will be your father, and you will be my sons and daughters, says the Lord Almighty". Dear friends, we have these promises from God, so we should make ourselves pure – free from anything that makes body or soul unclean. We should try to become holy in the way we live, because we respect God. (New Century Bible)

You will find that as you get deeper in your walk with God, you will not be very comfortable in the company of your old unbelieving friends and associates. You will discover that some of the things they do will no longer be attractive to you. Therefore, it is important that you try and establish new relationships in the church where you belong. Only attending 'church' on a Sunday morning will not enable you establish such friendships, as you would only meet people once a week.

RELATIONSHIPS   **40**

Notes

1. Make a list of your closest friends:

_____

_____

_____

_____

_____

_____

2. Which ones do you think will help you become a better Christian?

_____

_____

_____

_____

_____

_____

_____

YOUR NEW LIFE

41

3. What do you intend to do about those relationships that may not be helping your spiritual growth?

_____

_____

_____

_____

_____

4.   Write down the names of your family and friends you would like to see saved:

_____

_____

_____

_____

5. What steps do you intend to take to see that they get saved?

_____

_____

_____

5
SHARE YOUR FAITH

I mentioned earlier about the need for you to tell others about your new found faith in Christ. Why is this necessary? Well, nobody keeps any good news to himself/ herself. Just as you heard the good news and got saved, you need to help others find it too. The best thing you can do for anyone you truly love is to help them to escape the wrath and the judgement of God on those who reject His love. The reason some are not saved is because they do not understand what it is to be saved or indeed how it is that one can get saved. I will never forget an experience I had many years ago when a friend who had gotten saved confronted me. She said that I never really told her what it meant to be saved, I just assumed that she knew. Thank God she did not have to point that accusing finger at me before God. Someone had given her the simple message of salvation and she got saved and was enjoying her new found faith. We can see this example in John 1:35-50. There are so many ways we can share our faith with others.

Your Lifestyle
Firstly, let your friends and those around you see that you are not the same person you used to be. That itself is a witness, because if anyone is in Christ, he or she is a new creature; old things have passed away, and everything becomes new.

In Matthew 5:16 Jesus says "you are the light of the world". You are to let your light shine so that others will see your good works and glorify your Father in heaven. He also says "you are

YOUR NEW LIFE 43

the salt of the earth", (Matthew 5:13). What does salt do? It gives taste to our food. These verses of scripture suggest that as a new believer in Christ you are to be a good example to those around you. Let your life be attractive to them so they would want to find out more about your new faith.

Secondly, tell them how to get saved. Remember I said it was as simple as A,B,C,D.

Help them to pray to invite Jesus into their lives.

The Bible says that anyone who "turns a sinner from the error of his way will save a soul from death and cover a multitude of sins" (James 5:20).

Just as no married woman would like to remain barren in the natural, so also it is in the spiritual. As a believer, you are the Bride of Christ; your life is meant to be fruitful. Jesus wants us to help others to find Him.

How can you be fruitful? It is by abiding in Christ (see John 15: 1-16).

You also need to know that, *"he who is wise captures human lives (for God, as a fisher of men- he gathers and receives them for eternity)"* Proverbs 11:30 (Amplified Bible).

6
ONE WITH CHRIST

WATER BAPTISM

As a new believer, you have become one with Christ. One of the ways we identify with Christ is through his death and resurrection. This is symbolized through water baptism. After His death and resurrection, Jesus commanded His disciples to go into the world and preach the gospel to every creature. He who believes and is baptized will be saved, but he who does not believe will be condemned (Mark 16:16). And in Matthew 28:19 the same command is repeated: *"go therefore and make disciples of all the nations, baptizing them in the name of the father and of the son and the Holy Spirit"*.

One thing about Jesus is that He always shows us a good example of whatever He is asking us to do. Hence, although He was the Son of God, He too was baptized by John the Baptist at the river Jordan (see Matthew 3:13 -17). Hence Romans 6:1 -14 says

YOUR NEW LIFE

"What shall we say (to all this)? Are we to remain in sin in order that God's grace (favour and mercy) may multiply and overflow? Certainly not! How can we who died to sin live in it any longer? We were buried therefore with Him by the baptism into death, so that just as Christ was raised from the dead by the glorious (power) of the Father, so we too might (habitually) live and behave in newness of life. For if we have become one with Him by sharing a death like His, we shall also be (one with Him in sharing) His resurrection (by a new life lived for God). We know that our old (unrenewed) self was nailed to the cross with Him in order that (our) body (which is the instrument) of sin might be made no longer the slave of sin. For when a man dies he is freed (loosed, delivered) from (the power of sin (among men). Now if we have died with Christ, we believe that we shall also live with Him, because we know that Christ (the anointed one), being once raised from the dead, will never die again; death no longer has power over Him. For by the death He died, He died to sin (ending His relation to it) once for all; and the life that He lives, He is living to God (in unbroken fellowship with Him). Even so consider yourself also dead to sin and your relation to it broken, but alive to God (living in unbroken fellowship with Him) in Christ Jesus. Let not sin therefore rule as king in your mortal (short – lived, perishable) bodies, to make you yield to its cravings and be subject to its lusts and evil passions. Do not continue offering or yielding your bodily member (and faculties) to sin as instruments (tools) of wickedness. But offer and yield yourself to God as though you have been raised from the dead to (perpetual) life, and your bodily members (and faculties) to God, presenting them as implements of righteousness. For sin shall not (any longer) exert dominion over you, since now you are not under law (as slave), but under grace (as subjects of God's favour and mercy) (Amplified Bible).

THE LORD'S SUPPER

Before his crucifixion, Jesus shared supper with His disciples (Matthew 26: 26-29). *As they sat at the table, Jesus took bread, blessed and broke it, and gave it to the disciples and said, "take eat; this is my body ". Then He took the cup, and gave thanks, and gave it to them, saying, "drink from it, all of you, "for this is my blood of the new covenant, which is shed for many for the remission of sins." Jesus said to them "do this in remembrance of me"* (Luke 22: 19). Every time you partake of the Lord's Supper, you identify with His death and resurrection and remember the incredible sacrifice He made to redeem you from your sins.

In 1 Corinthians 11: 26 -29 the Bible says, *"for as often as you eat this bread and drink this cup, you are representing and signifying and proclaiming the fact of the lord's death until He come (again). So then whoever eats the bread or drinks the cup of the Lord in a way that is unworthy (of Him) will be guilty of (profaning and sinning against) the body and blood of the Lord. Let a man (thoroughly) examine himself, and (only when he has done) so should he eat of the bread and drink of the cup. For anyone who eats and drinks without discriminating and recognizing with due appreciation that (it is Christ's) body, eats and drinks a sentence (a verdict of judgment) upon himself"* (Amplified Bible).

YOUR NEW LIFE

As a new believer, remember to share communion (the Lord's Supper) with God's people as often as possible. When you do this, you are not only obeying His command, but identifying with His death and resurrection.

Notes

Baptism

1. If you desire to be baptized, you will need to find out from the leaders of the church you attend how to go about it. Make a note of the name and contact details of the person you need to see about it here:

_____

_____

_____

_____

2. If a date for the baptismal service has been fixed, write it here. Or if you have already been baptized make a note of the date:

_____

_____

_____

_____

ONE WITH CHRIST

3. Start to prepare yourself for your baptism, if you are not already baptized. Make a note of what you need to do. Some churches have preparatory classes to enable you understand the full meaning of baptism. Make every effort to attend these classes

_____

_____

_____

_____

4. Write down the names of family members and friends you would like to invite to your baptism:

_____

_____

_____

The Lord's Supper or Holy Communion

1. Find out how often the church you attend serves Holy Communion and make a note of it here:

_____

_____

YOUR NEW LIFE

2. Make every effort not to miss communion if you can help it. What adjustments do you need to make?

7
YOU SHALL RECEIVE POWER

The engine of a car is what gives it the power to operate, so also the Holy Spirit gives power to the believer to enable him or her live the Christian life. Without the power of the Holy Spirit in our lives, we cannot be effective in our witness for Christ. This was evident in the lives of the early Disciples of Christ. Although they had spent time with Jesus being taught by Him over the three years of His ministry and witnessed all the miracles He performed, they could not stand in the face of temptation. They had promised to follow Jesus to the very end, even unto death (see Matthew 26: 31-75). But for fear of their lives the disciples forsook Jesus when He needed them most.

Before His crucifixion, Jesus told His disciples that it was necessary for Him to die and that He would come back to life (that is, be resurrected) after 3 days. He assured them that when He was gone, He would send them the Holy Spirit to be with them forever. So, today, even though Jesus is not physically with us, He is represented through the Holy Spirit.

YOUR NEW LIFE

51

Hence, before He went to heaven, Jesus said to His disciples "but you shall receive power when the Holy Spirit has come upon you; and you shall be witnesses to Me in Jerusalem, and in all Judea and Samaria, and to the end of the earth " (Acts 1:8). This happened on the day of Pentecost (Acts 2), when all the disciples were gathered "with one accord in one place' (verse 1)'. "Then there appeared to them divided tongues as of fire, and one sat upon each of them. And they were all filled with the Holy Spirit and began to speak with other tongues, as the Spirit gave them utterance" (Acts 2: 3-4)

The interesting thing about this out–pouring of the Holy Spirit is that the apostles received power, just as Jesus had foretold. The next thing that happened was that the apostles became very bold in their witness. This is what the Holy Spirit will do for you.

When Jesus was facing His trials, before He was crucified on the cross, Peter denied Him three times. But this same Peter, when full of the Holy Spirit was able to stand publicly, unafraid, to preach the gospel to all the Jews that had gathered, having witnessed this out –pouring of the Holy Spirit. And in one day, about three thousand souls got saved (Acts 2: 41). This is what the Holy Spirit will do in your life. He will give you boldness to openly share your faith (see Acts 4: 13) and enable you live a more fulfilling life as a Christian.

Ask, and You Shall Receive

If you want the power of the Holy Spirit in your life, you need to sincerely ask for it. He does not force himself upon us. This is why Jesus declared in Luke 11 : 13 "if you then being evil , know how to give good gifts to your children , how much more will your heavenly father give the Holy Spirit to those who ask him!"

"So I say to you, ask, and it will be given to you; seek, and you will find; knock, and it will be opened to you" (Luke 11: 9) (New King James Bible).

Notes

1. Would you like to experience the Baptism of the Holy Spirit? Make a note here of why you feel you need this baptism and what steps you plan to take to make it happen:

_____

_____

_____

_____

_____

_____

"But you shall receive power when the Holy Spirit has come upon you; and you shall be witnesses to me in Jerusalem, and in Judea and Samaria, and to the end of the earth"
(Acts 1: 8)

8
RUN, FIGHT ... TO WIN

As a Christian, your walk with God is described in so many ways. The following are just a few:

A Race
Every year in England, the 'BUPA Great North Run' takes place in which thousands of people take part in a marathon. Besides the 'Great North Run', we also have the 'London Marathon', the Great South Run', and others. The interesting thing about these runs is that some start and complete successfully; others fail to do so. As a matter of fact, some people lose their lives during some of these runs. In addition to deaths, there are often casualties – those who get injured, faint, and so on. However, ONE person always emerges as the winner.

The Christian race is described in 1 Corinthians 9: 24 – 27 as follows:
You know that in a race all the runners run, but only one gets the prize. So run to win! All those who compete in the games use self-control so they win a crown. That crown is an

earthly thing that lasts only a short time, but our crown will never be destroyed. So I do not run without a goal. I fight like a boxer who is hitting something – not just the air. I treat my body hard and make it my slave so that I myself will not be disqualified after I have preached to others.

Also 2 Timothy 2: 5 says

An athlete who takes part in a contest must obey all the rules in order to win. The farmer who works hard should be the first person to get some of the food that was grown. (New Century Bible)

This is how it is in your walk with God. As a new believer, you are in a race and you must run to win. As you strive to win, the devil will do all he can to get you distracted; but you must remain focused, like an athlete.

Warfare

You will recall that I mentioned earlier that since you have left the enemy's camp, he will do everything to get you back. So, you will be in a constant battle everyday. And do not allow yourself to be deceived; the devil is very smart. He will come in so many different ways; hence like a soldier in battle, you need to be on your guard 24/7. No battle or warfare is easy, but you are encouraged to *"endure hardship as a good soldier of Jesus Christ"* (2 Timothy 2: 3).

More importantly, 2 Timothy 2: 4 says *"no one engaged in warfare entangles himself with the affairs of this life, that he may please Him who enlisted him as a soldier"*.

Your Spiritual Armour

Whereas soldiers in battle are faced with a real enemy they can see, your warfare is a spiritual one (see Ephesians 6:12). In other words you are fighting an enemy you cannot see physically. Nevertheless, the admonition to you in Ephesians 6:10 is to "be strong in the Lord and in the power of His might".

When soldiers go to war, they are fully equipped with all they would need. Similarly, the Bible tells you about your spiritual armour – the full gear you need to help you win this war. You are to "take up the whole armour of God, ..." Ephesians 6:13

Here is the list of your armour (Ephesians 6: 14–18; the New Century Bible)

- The belt of truth around your waist
- The protection of right living around your chest
- The Good News of peace on your feet to help you stand strong
- The shield of faith...
- The helmet of salvation...
- The sword of the Spirit – the word of God
- Praying always in the spirit... (your bullets)

Your goal in this battle is to overcome against all odds, for Jesus says, "he who overcomes will receive a crown of life" (Revelation 2:10)

There are also a lot of passages in the Bible that will help you understand what the kingdom of God is likened as:

- A Sower Matthew 13:3-23
- Wheat and Tares – Matthew 13:24-30 ; 37-43
- Mustard seed – Matthew 13:31-32
- Heaven – Matthew 13:33-
- Treasure hidden in a field – Matthew 13:44-
- Pearl of Great Price – Matthew 13:45-46
- Fishing Net – Matthew 13:47-50

What you need to understand is that you are an heir of God's kingdom and you need to do everything you can to remain a worthy member of that kingdom.

YOUR NEW LIFE

Notes

1. This Chapter has touched on some very important aspects of how to win the race or fight as a Christian. Make a note of specific things you have learnt:

2. What have you learnt concerning your Christian life from the following parables of Jesus:

   ### *The Sower: Matthew 13: 3-20*

Wheat and Tares: Matthew 13:24-30; 37-43

Mustard seed: Matthew 13: 31-32

Leaven: Matthew 13: 33

YOUR NEW LIFE

Treasure hidden in a field: Matthew 13: 44

Pearl of Great Price: Matthew 13: 45-46

RUN, FIGHT ... TO WIN

Fishing Net: Matthew 13: 47-50

9
EXTEND THE KINGDOM... THROUGH GIVING

As a member of God's family, you are to work hard to help extend the kingdom of your Heavenly Father here on earth. The point is that God cannot physically come down to the world to get people saved and to establish His kingdom on this earth. He has already sent Jesus into the world to show us what He expects of us. He expects us to use our resources to build and extend His kingdom in this world.

Genesis 28: 22 establishes the principle of tithing. Here it says *"of all you give me I will surely give a tenth to you"*.

The body of Christ to which you belong cannot operate effectively if believers do not give. So, we see the example of how the children of Israel brought everything that was needed to build the Tabernacle. The important thing was that they gave with a willing heart. (See Exodus 35; 2 Chronicles 31).

In Malachi 3:10-12 the Bible says *"Bring all the tithes (the whole tenth of your income) into the storehouse, that there may be food in My house, and prove Me now by it, says the Lord of hosts, if I will not open the windows of heaven for you and pour you out a blessing, that there shall not be room enough to receive it.*

And I will rebuke the devourer (insects and plagues) for your sakes and he shall not destroy the fruits of your ground, neither shall your vine drop its fruit before the time in the field, says the Lord of hosts.

And all nations shall call you happy and blessed, for you shall be a land of delight, says the Lord of hosts" (Amplified Bible).

As you sow into God's kingdom, He will bless you beyond measure. And as you "seek first His Kingdom and His righteousness" every other thing will be added to you. (Matthew 6:33)

It is the amount of seed that a farmer plants that will determine the type of harvest he will expect. This is known as the law of sowing and reaping. The more you give for God's work, by faith, the more He will bless you.

YOUR NEW LIFE

Notes

What you give for God's work is a matter between you and God. You might wish to make a note here about how you want to ensure you are sowing into God's kingdom:

10
THE OLD AND THE NEW LIFE

Throughout the earlier chapters of this book, I have drawn your attention to the fact that having prayed and invited Jesus to be the Lord over your life, you are now a child of God and a member of His holy family. As a member of the royal family of God, there are certain standards expected of you. Just as no member of the royal family either in the United Kingdom or elsewhere cannot afford to behave anyhow; so also it is with you. Now that you are a Christian, the Bible gives you guidance on how to live your life as a member of God's royal family.

The Way You Should Live

Ephesians 4:17-32 describes how God expects you to live your new life. It says

I tell you this in the name of the Lord: You must not live any longer like the people of the world who do not know God. Their thoughts are foolish. Their minds are in darkness. They are strangers to the life of God. This is because they have closed their minds to Him and have turned their hearts away from Him. They do not care anymore about what is right or wrong. They have turned themselves over to the sinful ways of the world and are always wanting to do every kind of sinful act they can think of. But you did not learn anything like this from Christ. If you have heard of Him and have learned

from Him, put away the old person you used to be. Have nothing to do with your old sinful life. It was sinful because of being fooled into following bad desires. Let your minds and hearts be made new. You must become a new person and be God-like. Then you will be made right with God and have a true holy life. So stop lying to each other. Tell the truth to your neighbour. We all belong to the same body. If you are angry, do not let it become sin. Get over your anger before the day is finished. Do not let the devil start working in your life. Anyone who steals must stop it! He must work with his hands so he will have what he needs and can give to those who need help. Watch your talk! No bad words should be coming from your mouth. Say what is good. Your words should help others grow as Christians. Do not make God's Holy Spirit have sorrow for the way you live. The Holy Spirit has put a mark on you for the day you will be set free. Put out of your life all these things: bad feelings about other people, anger, temper, loud talk, bad talk which hurts other people, and bad feelings which hurt other people. You must be kind to each other. Think of the other person. Forgive other people just as God forgave you because of Christ's death on the cross.
(Contemporary English Bible)

Our Bodies Are To Be a Living Gift

When we become born again, we are declaring that our lives no longer belong to us. In essence we give up our right to do whatever we please with our bodies, and offer it to God as a living sacrifice.

In Romans 12:1-2, the Bible says
Christian brothers (and sisters), I ask you from my heart to give your bodies to God because of His loving-kindness to us. Let your bodies be a living and holy gift given to God. He

THE OLD AND THE NEW LIFE

is pleased with this kind of gift. This is the true worship that you should give Him. Do not act like the sinful people of the world. Let God change your life. First of all, let Him give you a new mind. Then you will know what God wants you to do. And the things you do will be good and pleasing and perfect. (Contemporary English Bible)

Living in the Light

As a Christian, Jesus says, you are 'the light of the world' (Matthew 5: 14). What does this mean? How do we live in the light? This is well explained in Ephesians 5:1-14, which says

Imitate God, therefore, in everything you do, because you are his dear children. Live a life filled with love, following the example of Christ. He loved us[a] and offered himself as a sacrifice for us, a pleasing aroma to God.

Let there be no sexual immorality, impurity, or greed among you. Such sins have no place among God's people. Obscene stories, foolish talk, and coarse jokes—these are not for you. Instead, let there be thankfulness to God. You can be sure that no immoral, impure, or greedy person will inherit the Kingdom of Christ and of God. For a greedy person is an idolater, worshiping the things of this world.

Don't be fooled by those who try to excuse these sins, for the anger of God will fall on all who disobey him. Don't participate in the things these people do. For once you were full of darkness, but now you have light from the Lord. So live as people of light! For this light within you produces only what is good and right and true.

Carefully determine what pleases the Lord. Take no part in

YOUR NEW LIFE

the worthless deeds of evil and darkness; instead, expose them. It is shameful even to talk about the things that ungodly people do in secret. But their evil intentions will be exposed when the light shines on them, for the light makes everything visible. This is why it is said,

> *"Awake, O sleeper,*
> *rise up from the dead,*
> *and Christ will give you light."*

Living by the Spirit's Power

We cannot live in the light as we should in our own strength. The Holy Spirit enables us to do so. Hence Ephesians 5: 15-20 says

So be careful how you live. Don't live like fools, but like those who are wise. Make the most of every opportunity in these evil days. Don't act thoughtlessly, but understand what the Lord wants you to do. Don't be drunk with wine, because that will ruin your life. Instead, be filled with the Holy Spirit, singing psalms and hymns and spiritual songs among yourselves, and making music to the Lord in your hearts. And give thanks for everything to God the Father in the name of our Lord Jesus Christ. (New Living Version)

The New Life Lived by the Power of Christ

The power of God will enable you live a successful Christian life. As you daily trust Him, He will transform your mind and give you new desires and aspirations.

Colossians 3: 1-17 throws some light into this:

You have been raised to life with Christ. Now set your heart on what is in heaven, where Christ rules at God's right side. Think about what is up there, not about what is here on earth. You died, which means that your life is hidden with Christ, who sits beside God. Christ gives meaning to your life, and when He appears, you will also appear with Him in glory. Don't be controlled by your body. Kill every desire for the wrong kind of sex. Don't be immoral or indecent or have evil thoughts. Don't be greedy, which is the same as worshiping idols. God is angry with people who disobey Him by doing these things. And that is exactly what you did, when you lived among people who behaved in this way. But now you must stop doing such things. You must quit being angry, hateful, and evil. You must no longer say insulting or cruel things about others. And stop lying to each other. You have given up your old way of life with its habits. Each of you is now a new person. You are becoming more and more like your Creator, and you will understand Him better. It doesn't matter if you are a Greek or a Jew, or if you are circumcised or not. You may even be a barbarian or a Scythian, and you may be a slave or a free person. Yet Christ is all that matters, and He lives in all of us. God loves you and has chosen you as His own special people. So be gentle, kind, humble, meek, and patient. Put up with each other, and forgive anyone who does you wrong, just as Christ has forgiven you. Love is more important than anything else. It is what ties everything completely together.

YOUR NEW LIFE

Each one of you is part of the body of Christ, and you were chosen to live together in peace. So let the peace that comes from Christ control your thoughts. And be grateful.

Let the message about Christ completely fill your lives, while you use all your wisdom to teach and instruct each other. With thankful hearts, sing psalms, hymns, and spiritual songs to God. Whatever you say or do should be done in the name of the Lord Jesus, as you give thanks to God the Father because of him.

Notes

This chapter is probably one of the most important for you to remember. After reading this chapter, take time to reflect on the passages of scriptures that have been covered. Think of areas of your life that still need to be surrendered fully to God.

1. What are the things in your life that you have struggled with before you got 'born again'? For example, bad habits, wrong associations, etc. Write them here:

_____

_____

_____

_____

_____

THE OLD AND THE NEW LIFE

2. What changes have already taken place in your life since you got saved? Write them here:

_____

_____

_____

_____

_____

3. Make a note here of areas of your life that still need to be changed. Are there still any old sins, habits, etc. that you are still struggling with? Write them here:

_____

_____

_____

_____

4. Do you have people in your life that you need to forgive, or apologise to? Make a note of them here:

_____

_____

YOUR NEW LIFE

5. What steps are you going to take to put these wrongs right?

11
HOW TO DEAL WITH TEMPTATION

One thing you need to be aware of as a believer is that you would face a real struggle to go back to your old way of doing things. Friends, family, and others around you may think you have gone nuts and try to put pressure on you to conform. The pressure is not going to go away and sometimes you would almost be tempted to give in...do not lose heart! You are not alone in this. We all face temptations everyday. However, we have some great examples in the Bible of how to overcome temptations. Can you believe that even Jesus, the Son of God, our Saviour, was tempted? If He was, then you can be sure that you are not exempt. He has left us an example to follow in His footsteps; so we would know how to deal with temptation.

The Example of Jesus

In Matthew 3, we see how after Jesus was baptized, the heaven's opened and a voice was heard which said "This is my beloved Son, in whom I am well pleased". The next thing we see in Chapter 4 is that Jesus was led into the wilderness to be tempted by the devil. There was no physical devil standing in front of Him; these were the thoughts that were going through His mind. In the same way you will be faced with the battle of the mind, the struggle we all face everyday in which we will hear many voices trying to pull us in several directions. Sometimes the devil can also come to us through people, whom he uses as agents. No matter how he comes, you need to resist him, as James 4: 7 and 1 Peter 5: 9 say, and learn from the example of Jesus.

The temptations He faced were directed at making Him to abuse His position as the Son of God. You must realize that Jesus was in a very vulnerable position, like you will face sometimes. He had fasted for 40days and 40 nights and was very hungry. What was wrong with just commanding stones to become bread? He had the power to do so, didn't He? But He chose not to. Instead He said to the devil *"man shall not live by bread alone"*.

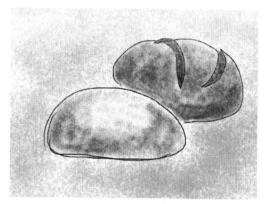

Jesus' response here is very significant. Firstly, Jesus was making it clear to the devil that our existence is not dependent on what is only physical. We are in this world not to be controlled by our fleshly appetites and desires, but by the Word of God. The Word of God is food for the soul as we examined earlier.

Secondly, Jesus was also making it clear to the devil that he was not in any position to tell Him what to do. In other words, Jesus was saying "hey devil, I take my instructions from God and not from you. I exist to do only what God says". This is very important for you as a believer. The decisions you will make everyday will depend on whose voice you are listening to – God's or the devil's.

In the second temptation as recorded in Matthew 4, the devil took Jesus up into the holy city and set Him on the pinnacle of the temple and told Him to cast himself down if He was the Son of God, since God had promised Him protection.

What a foolish thing to ask someone to do. As foolish as it may sound, some people would have fallen into such temptation – just to prove a point. You have nothing to prove to anyone. Sometimes your friends will put pressure on you to try to get you to do some things just to prove to them that you are now a different person. You do not have to yield to such temptations. The interesting thing in this temptation is that the devil was quoting the Bible, so, this is a trap you need to be aware of. You need to get to know your Bible very well so that you can distinguish between the voice of God and the voice of the devil. Jesus simply said to him, *"It is written, you shall not tempt the Lord your God"*. That suggests that you must not do anything foolish just to see if your God is real or not. He is real! And He does not expect us to put ourselves in the path of danger to prove that.

The story is told about a so-called prophet in Nigeria who was trying to prove to everyone that he was a prophet and just as God delivered Daniel from the mouth of lions, God would deliver him. So he threw himself into a den of lions and of course he was devoured. He made himself a free lunch for hungry lions. If he knew his Bible well he would have realized that Daniel did not cast himself into the den of lions (read Daniel chapter 6), others did that to him to punish him for serving God. In that situation of course, God had to prove that He was God and will deliver those who are faithful to him.

In the third and final temptation recorded in Matthew 4, the devil took Jesus up a high mountain and showed Him all the kingdoms of the world and their glory, and said to Jesus *"All these things I will give to you if you will fall down and worship me"*. Now, Jesus was quite angry and told the devil *"get away from my sight because it is written in God's word that we are to only worship and serve God"*. Now, this temptation is a very important one and this is where many Christians have fallen prey to the devil. This temptation can come very cunningly and suddenly. Sometimes we can allow ourselves to get carried away by the distractions of our jobs, businesses, wealth etc. The devil can get us so pre-occupied with these things that we do not have time to serve God. Here Jesus is trying to help us to see that whilst there is nothing wrong with us pursuing our jobs and careers, nothing must take the place of God in our lives. God and Him only should be worshipped!

HOW TO DEAL WITH TEMPTATION

One thing you would have noticed in all of Jesus' response to the devil is that He used the scriptures. Every time the devil made a suggestion to Him, He said "it is written". If Jesus, the sinless Son of God studied the Bible, then we ought to do the same, and more so too!

It is possible for one to think that it was easy for Jesus to overcome temptations, after all He is the Son of God. Now let us examine another person in the Bible who helps us to understand how to deal with temptation.

The Example of Joseph

You may or may not have heard about him; however the story of Joseph is a very famous one in the Bible. You can find out more about the life of this young man by reading Genesis chapters 37-50.

Joseph was the 11th son of his father Jacob, and his father loved him and made him a coat of many colours. His other brothers envied him because of this. To make matters worse, Joseph had a dream, which he shared with his family. This made them hate him the more. The dream appeared as though he was going to rule over the rest of the family and that they would all bow down to him. The opportunity came when at the age of 17years his father sent him to the field to seek out the welfare of his brothers who were caring for their father's flock. When they saw Joseph, they thought it was an opportunity to get rid of him – kill him, and then they would see what would become of his dream. But God did not allow Joseph to be killed. Instead, they beat and cast him into a pit. They then sold him off as a slave to some Ishmaelite traders from Egypt and told their father he had been devoured by a beast; having soaked his coat in animal blood they had killed.

Joseph was taken to Egypt and ended up in the house of Potiphar, the Captain of the guard of Pharaoh, king of Egypt. God was with Joseph and gave him favour in the home of Potiphar. Potiphar put everything in his house in Joseph's care; but because he was a very handsome young man, Potiphar's wife lusted after him. The young man was put under incredible pressure. Everyday she put pressure on him to have sex with her. Joseph's reply in Genesis 39:9 is worth noting. He said to his master's wife "There is no one greater in this house than I, nor has he kept back anything from me but you, because you are his wife. HOW THEN CAN I DO THIS GREAT WICKEDNESS, AND SIN AGAINST GOD?" The fear of God was the key for Joseph.

In Proverbs 29: 25, the Bible says *"The fear of man brings a snare, but whoever trusts in the Lord shall be safe"*. Imagine how many men would have fallen into the trap, which Potiphar's wife laid for Joseph. The opportunity even came when it was just both of them in the house and she grabbed Joseph by his shirt telling him to lie with her. What did he do instead? He left his shirt in her hand and she used it to lie against Joseph, which led to him being put in prison. She used her position to lie against an innocent person, but God was with Joseph and it was only a matter of time and the truth came to light. Even in prison God was with Joseph. And two years later, he became the Prime Minister of Egypt. Perhaps this would never have happened if Joseph had compromised his integrity.

This young man has left us a perfect example of what to do in the face of temptations – run for your life! There is a lovely hymn written by H.R. Palmer in 1897, which goes like this:

Yield not to temptation, for yielding is sin,
Each vict'ry will help you some other to win;
Fight manfully onward, dark passions subdue,
Look ever to Jesus, He'll carry you through

Ask the Saviour to help you,
Comfort, strengthen and keep you,
He is willing to aid you,
He will carry you through

YOUR NEW LIFE

Shun evil companions, bad language disdain,
God's Name hold in rev'rence, nor take it in vain;
Be thoughtful and earnest, kind hearted and true,
Look ever to Jesus, He'll carry you through

To him that o'ercometh God giveth a crown;
Thro' faith we shall conquer, tho' often cast down;
He who is our Saviour, our strength will renew,
Look ever to Jesus, He'll carry you through.

We now live in a world where wrong seems right; where it is okay to do what you like as long as you are happy with it. One with God is always in the majority, and doing the wrong thing because everyone is doing it, does not make it right. In Matthew 7: 13 -14, the Bible says "enter through the narrow gate. The gate is wide and the road is wide that leads to hell, and many people enter through that gate. But the gate is small and the road is narrow that leads to true life. Only a few people find that road" (New Century Bible).

And 1 Peter 5: 8, 9 says "be well balanced (temperate, sober of mind), be vigilant and cautious at all times; for that enemy of yours, the devil, roams around like a lion roaring (in fierce hunger), seeking someone to seize upon and devour" (Amplified Bible).

As you focus your attention on Jesus and on His word and seek to follow His example, you will find it much easier to deal with temptation. And remember that in 1 Corinthians 10: 13 the Bible promises not to allow you to be tempted beyond your strength; God will make a way of escape for you.

HOW TO DEAL WITH TEMPTATION 80

Notes

We all face temptations in many areas of our lives.

1. Make a note here of the areas you feel you are tempted the most?

_____

_____

_____

2. Write down what steps you plan to take to make sure you do not keep falling into the same temptations?

_____

_____

_____

_____

_____

_____

_____

YOUR NEW LIFE

12
GETTING BACK YOUR FIGHT

Let's face it, your number one enemy, the devil is very smart. In fact he is smarter than you can ever imagine. This is why he was able to deceive Eve (Genesis Chapter 3) into disobeying God. So, it is possible that sometimes even when you try so hard you may be overcome because the enemy has tricked you into committing a sin or doing something for which you are later ashamed. Do not be discouraged. Do not give up your fight. In Proverbs 24:16 the Bible says that the righteous man falls seven times and rises up again. Therefore if you find yourself in this situation do not waist any time; cry out to God quickly, repent and ask for His forgiveness. This is why 1 John 1: 8 says "'... If we confess our sins He is faithful and just to forgive us our sins and to cleanse us from all unrighteousness." Whilst it is not God's desire that we fall into sin, He has also made a way of escape for us to come back to Him. But this is not an excuse for us to keep on living in sin.

In I John 2:1-2, the bible declares
"My little children, these things I write to you, so that you may not sin. And if anyone sins, we have an Advocate with the Father, Jesus Christ the righteous. And He Himself is the propitiation for our sins, and not for ours only but also for the whole world".

The Test of Knowing Him

What is the true test that we know Him? It is in obeying Him and doing what He says. 1 John 2: 3-6 says

Now by this we know that we know Him, if we keep His commandments. He who says, "I know Him," and does not keep His commandments, is a liar, and the truth is not in him. But whoever keeps His word, truly the love of God is perfected in him. By this we know that we are in Him. He who says he abides in Him ought himself also to walk just as He walked."

Also 1 John 3: 2-3 says

"Beloved, now we are children of God; and it has not yet been revealed what we shall be, but we know that when He is revealed, we shall be like Him, for we shall see Him as He is. And everyone who has this hope in Him purifies himself, just as He is pure".

Sin and the Child of God

1 John 3: 4-9 says

The person who sins breaks God's law. Yes, sin is living against God's law. You know that Christ came to take away sins and that there is no sin in Christ. So anyone who lives in Christ does not go on sinning. Anyone who goes on sinning has never really understood Christ and has never known Him

Dear children, do not let anyone lead you the wrong way. Christ is all that is right. So to be like Christ a person must do what is right. The devil has been sinning since the beginning, so anyone who continues to sin belongs to the devil. The Son of God came for this purpose to destroy the devil's work. Those

GETTING BACK YOUR FIGHT **84**

who are God's children do not continue sinning, because the new life from God remains in them. They are not able to go on sinning, because they have become children of God."

As you can see from these passages, it is God's desire that you do not give into sin but must always be on your guard as 1 Peter 5: 8-9 says *"Be sober, be vigilant, because your adversary, the devil, walks about like a roaring lion seeking whom he may devour. You are to resist him and remain steadfast in the faith."*

The difference between a pig and a sheep is this, when a sheep falls into the mare, it cries out for help because it knows that is not where it belongs. But when a pig falls into the mare, it sticks in there because that is where it belongs. Before you were saved you were like a sheep that went astray but now that you have invited Jesus into your life you are a sheep that has been redeemed through the precious blood of Jesus Christ our Lord and Savior. Therefore you do not belong to the mare and must be circumspect in your daily walk with God so that you do not fall into the mare and be tempted to remain there. The Bible says in 1Timothy 6: 12 *"Fight the good fight of faith and lay hold on eternal life to which you were also called"*. It is a fight that has been described as 'good' because our victory has been won for us on the Cross; so you must never give up your fight.

Remember, earlier we talked about the Christian armour (see Ephesians 6: 10-18). You must never be without your spiritual armour and thanks be to God who has assured us of victory through Christ Jesus, our Lord and Savior.

YOUR NEW LIFE

Notes

1. If you found yourself falling into sin after you got saved and are suffering from guilt, don't give up. You may want to seek godly counsel from your pastor, cell leader, or Christian mentor, and ask for prayers. But don't try to hide or cover up your sins. In Proverbs 28: 13, the Bible says 'if you hide your sins, you will not succeed. If you confess and reject them, you will receive mercy' (New Century Bible).

2. Make a note of specific steps you will take to avoid falling into deliberate sins.

13
PRAYER AND FASTING

The importance of prayer in the life of a Christian cannot be overemphasized. Earlier I mentioned that you should talk to your heavenly Father as often as possible. This is because the Bible urges us to 'pray without ceasing' (1 Thessalonians 5: 17). Jesus also told us in Luke 18:1 to 'always pray and never lose hope'. Prayer is the lifeline that links us to God. How can we make our needs known to God if we do not talk to Him? However, you will find that sometimes when you want to pray, your flesh and your spirit will be at war (Galatians 5: 17). You might want to pray, and you flesh will cry out 'I'm tired, I just want to go to bed'. What do you do when you find yourself struggling to find the time to pray? The devil will of course do everything within his power to stop you from praying. This is where you need to set specific time apart to pray.

Fasting is a special time that a Christian sets aside to focus on God for various reasons. The Bible is replete with examples of different types of fasts, and why people fasted. This is such a huge (and sometimes controversial) subject that I cannot go into too much details in this book. However, fasting helps us to pray more effectively, as we give up our right to food and other pleasures to focus on spiritual matters.

Jesus never asks us to do anything that He himself did not

do. He left us an ex ample to follow in His footsteps. Before He began His earthly ministry, after His baptism, he went into the wilderness and fasted for forty days and forty nights. Why? It was to prepare Him for the work he had to do. He was aware of the huge task ahead of Him, including the journey to the Cross.

There numerous examples of others in the Bible who show us the various reasons why we need to fast:

1. When we have an important assignment to fulfill and we need God's power and grace to accomplish it (see the example of Moses in Exodus 24:18 and 34: 28; Elijah in 1 Kings 19).
2. When we face a difficult situation or a big problem for which we need special deliverance (see Esther chapters 3 to 7; 2 Samuel 12; Mark 9: 29).
3. When we want to draw closer to God and build an intimate relationship with God (Daniel 9; Psalm 35: 13; Psalm 69: 10; 1 Corinthians 7: 5).

Fasting brings a certain amount of discipline into our lives as Christians, as we make certain sacrifices because we love God and want to serve Him no matter what it takes. As a new believer, one of the ways you can grow into a strong and mature Christian is to cultivate the habit of praying regularly, including some element of fasting. Your spiritual mentor will be able to give you further guidance on this subject.

PRAYER AND FASTING

Notes

1. Most Bible-believing churches have certain times set aside for their members to fast. Try and join in as much as possible.

_____

_____

_____

_____

2. Study some of the examples of people who fasted in the Bible and make a note of the specific reasons why these fasts were necessary.

_____

_____

_____

_____

_____

_____

YOUR NEW LIFE

89

3. What steps do you plan to take to ensure you build in regular periods of fasting into your Christian life?

14
KEYS FOR SUCCESSFUL CHRISTIAN LIVING

If you cannot remember everything in this book, here are a few important principles you need to remember:

1. You are a new person in Christ. Live as one who belongs to God's family. Do not do anything that will displease God.
2. Read your bible everyday. Mark and memorize the Scriptures. Live on the Word of God – Blessed are they that hear the Word of God and keep it.
3. Spend much time in secret prayer. Prayer changes things. Have a prayer list. Pray the prayer of faith. Claim the answer in advance. Fast when necessary.
4. Share your faith at every opportunity. Don't be ashamed of Jesus. Try to win others to Christ. Tell others how Jesus saved you. Take guests, family or friends to Church with you.
5. Attend all the church services and fellowship meetings possible. Don't let any excuse keep you away. You might miss great blessings.
6. Trust God completely. Christians should not worry. All things work together for good to those who love God. Trust in the Lord at all times.
7. Use your talents and resources to serve and honour God. He gave you these gifts to use for His glory.
8. Honour God with your tithes. The tithe is the Lord's and

is holy (Leviticus 27: 30). Bring all the tithes into God's storehouse. Superabundance is promised for obedience. (Proverbs 3: 9-10).

9. You are in a spiritual battle with an enemy 24/7. Do not allow yourself to be taken unawares. Always be on your guard.
10. Never take off your spiritual armour (Ephesians 6: 10-18).
11. Do not yield to temptation. Avoid ungodly relationships and associations.
12. Desire to please God in every area of your life. Be a committed and faithful Christian.
13. Think positively at all times, and have fervent faith in God. Be full of hope and do not despair. Never give up.
14. God loves you and has promised never to leave or forsake you. He is with you always.

Make these scriptures part of your life daily. Affirm them aloud in faith.

1. The Lord is the strength of my life (Psalm 27: 1).
2. I am more than a conqueror through Christ (Roman 8: 37).
3. My God shall supply all my need (Philippians 4: 19).
4. Sin shall have no dominion over me (Romans 6: 14).
5. I overcome the devil by the Blood of Jesus (Revelation 12: 11) .
6. The Just shall live my faith (Hebrews 10: 38).
7. The love of God is shed abroad in my heart (Romans 5: 5).

KEYS FOR SUCCESSFUL CHRISTIAN LIVING

Notes

Make a note of things you have learnt from this section

15
WHERE TO FIND HELP

When in fear
- *"Fear not, I am with you; be not afraid, I am your God"* (Isaiah 41:10).

- *"The Lord is my light and my salvation whom shall I fear"* (Psalm 27:1).

- *"Whenever I am afraid I will trust in you"* (Psalm 56:3).

- *"God has not given us the Spirit of fear, but of power, love and of a sound mind"* (2 Timothy 1:7).

When anxious
- *"Be anxious for nothing, but in everything by prayer and supplication with thanksgiving let your requests be made known to God"* (Philippians 4:6).

- *"You will keep them in perfect peace whose heart is stayed on you because he trusts in you"* (Isaiah 26: 3).

- *"Cast all your cares upon Him because He cares for you"* (1 Peter 5: 7).

- *"Therefore I say to you, do not worry about your life, what you will eat or what you will drink; about your*

WHERE TO FIND HELP

body, what you will put on. Is not life more than food and the body more than clothing? (Matthew 6: 25).

In sickness

- *"I am the Lord who heals you"* (Exodus 15: 26).

- *"Bless the Lord, O my soul, and forget not all His benefits; who forgives all your iniquities, who heals all your diseases* (Psalm 103: 2-3).

- *"By His stripes you are healed"* (1 Peter 2: 24).

When in Need

- *"My God shall supply all my needs according to His riches in glory through Christ Jesus"* (Philippians 4: 19).

- *"The Lord is my Shepherd, I shall not want* (Psalm 23: 1).

- *"Therefore do not worry, saying, 'What shall we eat?' or 'What shall we drink?' or 'What shall we wear?'* (Matthew 6: 36).

- *"Therefore do not worry about tomorrow, for tomorrow will worry about its own things. Sufficient for the day is its own trouble* (Matthew 6: 36).

When lonely

- *"I am with you always, even to the end of the age"* (Matthew 28: 20).

- *"Never will I leave you; never will I forsake you"* (Hebrews 13: 5)

- *"So do not fear, for I am with you* (Isaiah 41: 10 and 43:5).

- *"The eternal God is your refuge, and underneath are the everlasting arms"* (Deuteronomy 33: 27).

- *"I will be with you; I will never leave you nor forsake you* (Joshua 1: 5).

When discouraged

- *"Do not be discouraged, for the LORD your God will be with you wherever you go"* (Joshua 1: 9).

- *"Do not be afraid; do not be discouraged"* (Deuteronomy 1: 21).

- *"You, who have shown me great and severe troubles, shall revive me again, and bring me up again from the depths of the earth. You shall increase my greatness, and comfort me on every side"* (Psalm 71: 20-21).

- *"Come, and let us return to the LORD; For He has torn, but He will heal us; He has stricken, but He will bind us up"* (Hosea 6: 1).

- *"Giving thanks always for all things to God the Father in the name of our Lord Jesus Christ"* (Ephesians 5: 20).

Notes

Make a note of things you have learnt from the book

YOUR NEW LIFE

Notes

Make a note of things you have learnt from the book

Notes

Make a note of things you have learnt from the book

Notes

Make a note of things you have learnt from the book

YOUR NEW LIFE

Notes

Make a note of things you have learnt from the book

ABOUT THE AUTHOR

Dr Elewechi Ngozi Okike is an inspirational writer, who works within the higher education sector. She has been in academia for over 35 years, and is passionate about making a difference to the lives of others through her personal experiences. This is reflected in all her writings.

Her desire to make a difference in the lives of others led to the establishment of BOOK AID FOR AFRICA, a Charity that is helping to address the imbalance in educational provision in Africa.

www.bookaidforafrica.com

BUY ONLINE AT
www.assurancepublications.com
www.amazon.co.uk
ORDER BY PHONE
0 8 4 5 2 9 9 1 1 2 7

Visit www.afexed.com/www.ngoziokike.com to find out more about Dr Okike's books and other aspects of her work. You can also join Dr Okike on Facebook, LinkedIn or follow her on twitter @ngozi0kike1

ALSO BY THE AUTHOR

The
Greatest Debtor
to His **Love**
and a Trophy of His Grace

- Stranger than fiction.
- Real and captivating!
- Highly inspirational and challenging.
- Unlocks secrets for overcoming obstacles and challenges
- Contains keys for WINNING in life.
- Sarah Hathaway of BBC Tyne describes Ngozi's life as 'very dramatic and eventful',

How does anyone survive abortion, escape rape, murder, abduction and overcome prejudice and injustice? Find out as you read this real life account of Elewechi Ngozi Okike in "The Greatest Debtor to His Love and a Trophy of His Grace".

This is a book that encourages one never to give up on one's dreams and aspirations, even in the face of persecution, no matter how long it takes. It is a compelling read, both in style and content.

ALSO BY THE AUTHOR

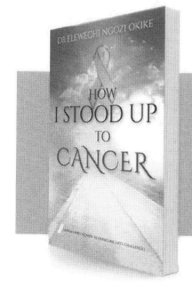

- Real and captivating!
- Highly inspirational, challenging and empowering
- Details the mental and physical impact of faith and positive mental attitude
- Empowers women to overcome life's challenges
- Former BBC Reporter, Sarah Hathaway, describes author's life as 'very dramatic and eventful'

HOW I STOOD UP TO CANCER provides a detailed account of a wife, mother and grandmother's shocking diagnosis of a rare and medically unique type of breast cancer; so rare that its discovery was asked to be published in the British Medical journal.

Read this book and journey with Dr Okike as she opens up about the intense mental, physical and spiritual battles she faced as she fought for her life.

This book is a celebration of life and a testament to the immense impact faith and a positive mental attitude can have on our well-being when applied to all aspects of life, especially through life's challenging moments.

Be empowered, be inspired, be your best ...

ALSO BY THE AUTHOR

- A captivating read!
- Highly inspirational
- Recognizing your 'God moment'
- Avoid presumptuousness
- There's nothing wrong with recognition
- Faith accomplishes the impossible
- Shine your light even in the darkest moments
- See beyond the veil; appearances are deceptive

Elewechi Ngozi Okike rejected an opportunity to be one of the Torch Bearers to carry the Olympic Torch, as part of the opening of the London 2012 Olympics. While she was musing over this decision, she suddenly found herself facing a breast cancer diagnosis. So, how do you shine your light and carry your torch for all to see in the face of a life-threatening disease?

Through the experiences shared in the book, Elewechi helps the reader to appreciate the importance and the significance of being 'Torch Bearers' even in the most difficult and dark places in life. She draws attention to the fact that our ability to shine our light at such times has a higher level impact than carrying the physical Olympic Torch.